*May life always offer a message of hope*

# Message *of* Hope

Inspirational Thoughts
for Uncertain Times

Kathleen Gage

Maxwell Publishing
Salt Lake City, Utah

Copyright © 2002 by Kathleen Gage
First Edition 2002
Manufactured in the United States of America

Cover illustration and image by
Karen Noel with contribution by Nettie Apland
© 2002 by Karen Noel. All Rights Reserved.

ISBN 0-9658159-4-3

1. Inspirational     2. Self-help

This book is dedicated to the loving memory of
Van Andreasen
1961 - 1998

Message of Hope is also dedicated to people
everywhere who have inspired me by their example
of courage to walk through challenging experiences
in life with dignity, integrity and love.

My most heartfelt thanks, appreciation, and love to Karen Noel, for helping me to believe in my dreams even when I can't; my mother and father for being my heroes and instilling values that I respect and appreciate; my sister Pat for your love, friendship and willingness to listen; my sister Lorraine for all you contribute to my life; Robert for the gift of friendship; Kathleen for showing me a life tragedy can be turned into the greatest blessing of our life; Patrick who is an amazing example of what it means to manifest our desires; and Nettie for teaching me that any mountain can be climbed one step at a time.

# *P*ersonal *N*ote

Some experiences constitute a turning point, or what is also known as a change of heart or perspective. Life is just a fleeting moment - it spins on a dime. Beliefs that are our guiding force can be stripped away in a moment. Change happens in an instant. Nothing is forever, little is for sure.

***Message of Hope*** was born out of an experience of great pain and yet, intense gratitude. Pain at the sudden passing of my dear friend, Van Andreasen at the age of 36, and gratitude at the blessing of his friendship. It was through the process of grieving and healing that ***Message of Hope*** unfolded.

# Forgiveness

Forgiveness is a step that will move me closer to my primary purpose in life, which is to be a loving person. It is difficult to be my most loving self if I am holding on to negative feelings about another person or a past or present situation. I allow myself to release any feelings I may have which do not serve my highest good or the highest good of others. I ask for the willingness to be the most loving way I can. I ask that I be shown how to truly forgive another against whom I may be holding angry feelings. It is in the forgiving that I can live life to the fullest.

# Confusion

---

When I am confused, I don't need to have all the answers to everything that happens in life. I can turn to others for their wisdom. Turning to another may seem to be a weakness to some. Yet true strength in life comes from knowing I don't have to do life on my own. True strength comes from reaching out my hand to another and letting others reach out to me.

---

# lness

---

When I am physically ill, the place to start my healing, the only place to heal, is in the mind and the spirit. For when the mind and the spirit are healed, the body heals. The process of healing is one of growth and learning. Growth within ourselves and learning how to fully accept what is and the love others will share with us.

---

# eath

---

When someone I love passes from life to death, it is okay for me to feel my pain. This pain is neither good nor bad; it just is. In allowing myself to feel my pain, I will find a deeper level of my love for others. It is also in the pain that I can begin my healing. I may not want to accept my loved one's passing, yet I know that their spirit has been guided to a safe and loving place.

---

# Resentment

Resentment is a powerful emotion that often destroys. I realize the need to release any and all resentment I may be holding onto. When I think life is unfair, without love and respect, it is up to me to find that place in myself that allows me to discover my own level of fairness, love and respect. Life works from the inside out, not the outside in. My experience of life is based on my experience of myself and the willingness to let go of resentment.

# nger

I may believe I have the right to get angry at others. What gives me the right? Anger is an emotion. It is neither right nor wrong, but what I do with it will make all the difference. If I am unsure of the most appropriate action to take around my anger, the best thing I can do is slow down, breathe and ask for guidance in order to release it.

# Remembering

For today, I will take time to remember special people who have touched my life. I will remember all the friends who have passed on. I will remember all the moments I have shared with those who have made a difference in my life. For today, I will realize how blessed I have been to have so many wonderful people touch my life. I will give thanks for all the special memories.

# Control

When I find myself trying to take control of the outcome of a situation, I will open my heart to the process of life. I will simply ask for the courage to trust the process. In trusting I gain insight into more of the meaning of life. Often the greatest control I can have is in the willingness to let go, be in the moment and trust the process before me.

# esson

---

Not everything is a lesson to be learned. Sometimes things simply happen as a part of the process of life. I can release the need to analyze every situation and simply be in the experience. It is by being with the experience of life, I can more easily accept all that is in front of me. For this I give thanks.

# Turning Points

There are some experiences in life which constitute a turning point for me. This I know to be true. Often I will intellectualize the experience and resist the change. The key to true growth is to take the change to heart. This is the purest type of turning point I can allow myself to experience. By allowing myself to be guided by the process of life, I find the turning points easier to embrace and accept.

# urpose

How often do I take my time on earth for granted? How often do I miss the power of the present moment? There is a purpose in each moment and a purpose for each of us. The simplicity of our purpose is to sincerely do the best we can do. I am constantly being shown what I am destined to do, yet my mind, ego or intellect can get in the way. I may try to analyze so much of what I experience rather than just living in the moment. The key to true serenity and happiness is to simply experience life as it unfolds.

# Change

Change is the natural order of life. Some change I willingly embrace. Other change I may be tempted to resist. When I get in the quiet place that allows me to listen to the process of life, I realize all transformation is a part of the master plan for my life and the lives of others. The more I embrace the change, the closer I can be to following my path.

# Death

When I experience the passing of people I love, I can turn my concern over to a power greater than myself to assist me in walking through my pain. With virtually every passing I experience, I can choose to resent what has happened or I can choose to truly be grateful for the time I was able to share with my loved ones. It is essential that I savor every day I have with those I love. The greatest gift I can give to others is the creation of loving memories.

# *E*xpectations

I may be hard on myself due to my expectations. For today I will be gentle to myself. When I find that I am having unrealistic expectations about who I think I should be or what I should have accomplished in my life by this point in time, I will take an imaginary step back and realize I am human. I don't have to be all things to all people. On some days the best that I can do is to suit up, show up and do the next indicated step. It may be something as simple as putting one foot in front of the other. For today, I will be gentle on myself and allow life to unfold in its natural order.

# Resistance

There are occasions where I may resist what is going on in my life because I think I know what is best for myself or others. By resisting what is, I experience unnecessary pain. I am, in essence, saying I do not trust life's plan. I have the choice to either resist or not. What I do know is that when I flow with what is, I can move through the difficult times with more dignity and ease. Moment by moment, my actions will have influence on the circumstances of my life. When I slow down, get quiet and allow myself to tune in to all that is occurring, I can see that everything is happening exactly as it should.

# *W*orry

How often do I miss the preciousness of life by worrying about what I did or did not do in the past, what I will or will not do in the future? To fully appreciate the wonders life has to offer, it is important for me to stay present in the moment. That does not mean I cannot plan for my future. It simply means that in all the best-laid plans, I must be willing to accept whatever life puts in my path. By reaching a deep level of acceptance of what is and not wasting time and energy on unnecessary worry, I am able to fully be in my life.

# Uncertainty

When I am uncertain about a situation, all I need to do is to take a quiet moment and listen to the answers that are inside me. Simply let go of the distractions that make it difficult to intuitively know the right action to take. In the quietness I can get the clarity I need to know what the next right action is to take. In some cases the best action will be no action.

# esentment

Sometimes I feel very blocked in life. Usually when I have these kinds of feelings it is because I am placing expectations on how I think a situation ought to be. When things don't turn out as I expected I may find myself moving into a place of resentment. I can choose to stay in these resentments or choose to handle the situation in a more loving way. I realize that life is too short to hold on to resentments that can eat at me. With kindness as my guide I can easily walk in love.

# *A*nger

If I am angry or hurt by what someone else may have said or done, my initial response may be to strike back to get even. Trying to get even does not solve anything. The anger can only bring more hurt. The best thing I can do is pray for the other person. Pray that they may have all the goodness that I would desire for myself and those I love. Through this action, the other person may not change, and yet, my feelings around the person and the situation will.

# Moving Forward

In order to move forward in my life in a happy, positive way I must be willing to let go of the past around those things which hold me back and hold me down. I must release any resentments I may be holding towards another and any anger I may be harboring towards a situation. I am determined to see things differently. I am determined to move forward. The first step is having the willingness to do things differently.

# Frustrations

---

There may be times I find myself getting irritated with little things. I have to ask myself, "Is it really worth getting upset about this? Is it worth it to get frustrated about things I have no control over?" During the times when I feel my anger rise I can get in a quiet space and ask for guidance. It is through quiet guidance that I can release all my hostility and anger. If I want peace, I must live peacefully. If I want love, I must live lovingly. If I want serenity, I must live serenely. Whatever it is I desire, I must be willing to live moment by moment.

---

# nxiety

If I find myself getting frustrated and anxious during the day I can simply close my eyes and visualize myself in a far away place for a moment of reprieve. In my mind I can find peace and serenity, joy and happiness, even during the trying times. I can choose to see myself taking a stroll along a quiet path. I can hear myself laughing with others. I can feel myself being loving with others. In my mind and heart I can find happiness. Anxiety will be replaced by happiness, love and joy.

# *F*ear

Fear often holds me back from doing what my heart desires. What one thing would I do if this were the only day I had left? In reality, today is the only day I have. What can I do, given my present circumstances, which will allow me to move closer to my heart's desire? Who would I contact to tell them how much I care? What experience would I share if today were my only day? What legacy would I leave behind?

# Irritations

---

Throughout the day there may be things that irritate me. If I find myself getting irritated at any point today, I will pause and remember to breathe. I will take the time to consciously slow down and ask for guidance. I will embrace my experiences, no matter how irritating. I will ask myself what it is about this situation that is not to my liking. As I become quiet I will notice what the next indicated step should be to move into a more accepting state.

---

# Gratitude

With each moment that passes, with each breath I take, I will give thanks for the experiences I am having. I will give thanks for the clouds in the sky, the wind in the trees, the birds in flight. I will give thanks for the ability to reason, to think and to understand. Most of all I will give thanks for the love I have to share and my willingness to open my heart to others.

# Confidence

Looking back over the experiences of my life I can now smile as I reflect on those times where I walked through extreme fear. I notice how much I grew during those times when I may not have had confidence, but I walked through the situation anyway. Now I know I have confidence in areas where in the past I had none. All I need to do is trust the process and know that with each day that passes I become a stronger and a more complete and capable human being.

# Understanding

I might not understand some of the things that happen in life, even as they are unfolding. I may not understand the pain or tragedy. Yet I can look over my entire life and realize that often the most tragic and desperate times were the most enlightening. They were the experiences that took me to the next level of connecting with my purpose in life.

# ove

I will send love to all I do and experience. Every person I come in contact with is an opportunity for me to love unconditionally. There may be times when I think my love should be reserved for those who "deserve" it. It is not my place to judge another's station in life. There is a plan for all of us and life's plan for me is that I learn to love unconditionally. Each moment of each day I have the opportunity to share love with the people I connect with in every situation. What I know is that the more love I give the more I am in a position to receive.

# Self Love

There will be times when life can be very overwhelming. I will give myself permission to realize that I will go through situations which can be very draining emotionally, physically and spiritually. It is okay for me to step back and retreat from the pressures around me. I will spend more time being loving and gentle to myself. Today I will do something nice for myself, instead of waiting for someone else to do so. I may take a walk in the park, buy myself flowers, write myself a letter or take a long, leisure bath. I will do what I need to do to feel loved, appreciated and whole.

# ear

There are times I may hold myself back from what I really want to do out of fear. Fear of rejection, failure, ridicule. Fear of joy, love, success. When I walk in the path of trust, fear will disappear from my life. Life will lead me to the avenues that I must go through to become the person I am intended to be. In each moment I have the opportunity to become who I am meant to be. In each moment I am where I am supposed to be. In each moment I can choose to let go of the fear and trust the process of life.

# indness

Kindness is a choice I make. There may be times I am tempted to be harsh due to the pressures of my day. In each moment I can make a choice to be kind or not. Today if I find myself getting harsh at any point, I will stop, breathe, and focus on my heart energy. I will consciously focus on being more loving and kind to all I come in contact with.

# $\mathscr{P}$urpose

I may think I know what my purpose in life is. If I am anxious and stressful about what I am doing then obviously I do not know my purpose. My only purpose is to be a loving human being. It is to walk in love. When I remember this all my fear, anxiety and stress will diminish.

# Compassion

There may be times I get upset by what another person is or isn't doing; is or isn't saying; is or isn't being according to my standards. The reality is that I am not the center of the universe! I don't know what that person may be going through. I may think they are not paying attention when I am talking to them and yet, it could be they just learned some very sad news that has them in a place of shock. Maybe they are not in a position to respond according to my standard at that moment. The most loving thing I can do is to try to understand what another is going through. The most loving thing I can do is to realize that everyone has something going on that I may not understand at that moment.

# ntimacy

When I am with people I love I will open my heart completely and let go of the fear of intimacy. Intimacy is the ability to be in the present and let others experience my essence. Intimacy is about letting go of the fear of people knowing who I truly am. Intimacy is one of the greatest gifts I can offer another. Intimacy simply means in-to-me-see.

# As I Am

I know I am a complete person as I am. I do not need to win awards, I do not have to bend to please others, I do not have to pretend to be something I am not. All I have to do is be true to who I am and know that this is good.

# Expression Of Good

Today I will take the time to acknowledge something good someone else has done. I will speak from my heart as I express my gratitude for what they have done. Though this may be uncomfortable for me, I will take the time to let another know how much I appreciate who they are. If I find this difficult I will pause, notice where my resistance is and realize the only moment I have is now.

# Gratitude

Often I spend precious time trying to figure out what I should be doing in life. The fact is that right now I am doing exactly what I should be at this moment in time. Whatever job I have, relationship I am in, home I live in, this is what is meant to be at this moment. These things may not always remain the same, but for now they are as they should be. As I become more in tune with the process of life, I will know all the right actions to take to move me to my next situation. The key is to be grateful for all the experiences I have.

# essings

When I feel sorry for myself for what I think I don't have, it is time for me to focus on what I do have. If I don't think I have a big enough house, a fast enough car, or the right designer clothes, it may be time for me to humble myself and acknowledge what I do have. Do I have my health? Do I have love from another? Do I have a roof over my head? Do I have food on my table? Do I have God in my life? When I can stop long enough to acknowledge what I do have, rather than what I don't, I can once again appreciate my path in life.

# ttitude

My attitude plays a big part in my enjoyment of life. Today I will focus on all the blessings I have been given, whether they are big or small. The more I focus on what is good the more abundance I will experience. The more I focus on the blessings in my life, the better my attitude will become.

# Giving Thanks

---

I give thanks for this day before me. I give thanks for the abundance I have been given, for the health I have and for all the love in my life. I give thanks for all my trials and pain, for without them I would not grow. Most of all I give thanks for the ability to acknowledge the importance of giving thanks.

---

# Nourishment

As much as my body is nourished by good food, it is also nourished by good thoughts. My thoughts are powerful forces in my life. If I have good thoughts my body, mind and spirit can stay balanced. I realize that what I put into my mind through what I read, talk about or hear makes a big difference in my emotional state. I will surround myself with good thoughts, readings and conversation. I will surround myself with loving and caring people. I will become nourished.

# Sending And Receiving

As I open my heart to the goodness of life, I attract more goodness. As I send more love to others, whether they be strangers or those I am familiar with, I receive more love. Whatever I put forward to others I will get more of. Today I will put forth more love, care and compassion. Today I will also be open to receiving the same.

# rust

As I am willing to trust the process of life, I know in my heart when I walk through one door and it closes, another will open. All I have to do is be present in the moment and trust that all is as it should be. Although this may be difficult at times, I can simply look back over my life and see that over and over this has proven to be true. For today, I will allow any doors to close in order for others to open.

# Loving One Another

Today I will do a good deed and not tell anyone what I have done. I may send an anonymous card to someone who is feeling unloved. Maybe pick up some trash left behind by another. Or buy a meal for a street person. Perhaps visit a hospital and stop in on a patient who has had no visitors. I need not let anyone know what I have done. On some occasions even the receiver need not know I was the giver of the gift. It is in the giving of myself in this fashion that I can truly stay humble.

# Right Time

All things will happen in their right time if I just let life flow as it should. The more I trust the process of life, the easier life becomes. Even during times of hardship, times when things are not appearing as they should, if I just step back and let life unfold all will turn out as it should.

# Today

Today is a new day. It doesn't matter what took place yesterday or what will happen tomorrow. In reality, this is the only day and moment I have. It is up to me to make each moment a good one with a special memory attached to it. My day is based not on the outward experiences, but rather on my attitude towards those experiences. May I fill my day with a grateful attitude and loving actions.

# nswers

How many people seem to think they can predict the future? How many people believe they have plenty of time to do what they want or need to do? In reality, none of us has anything beyond this moment in time. How often do I try to control the direction of my life? What I do have control over is my attitude, my willingness to be teachable and to admit that I may not have all the answers.

# Patience

There are times I may have tried to force the flow of situations. I became frustrated when things didn't turn out as I thought they should. And yet, as I look back on virtually every situation in which I became impatient, I can clearly see there was a reason for it not turning out as I had expected. In the future, when things are occurring in a way other than what I think they should be, I will pause and allow myself to come to a place of acceptance. By learning acceptance I will also gain patience.

# Trust

Trust is the key to my wisdom. I will learn to trust all that I am experiencing. Every situation is a perfect opportunity for me to evolve into the person I am intended to become. Each day I have an abundance of opportunities to be a loving and kind human being. Each moment I can move closer to my true purpose and live life fully.

# *C*onnecting

---

Time seems to pass so quickly. There is someone I have intended on making contact with for quite a while. Someone who I know would be as happy to hear from me as I would be to connect with them. I will take the time today to make a connection with this person. It could be through a letter, a phone call or an email. Regardless of the method, I commit to connect with them today.

---

# *R*outines

It is so easy to get stuck in my routines. Routines are safe and comfortable. Although some routines are appropriate, I know that at times it is very healthy to break out of others. It doesn't have to be anything drastic. It can be as simple as driving a different route to work or sitting in a different seat on the bus. It might be drinking my morning coffee with my left hand instead of my right. Perhaps getting up on the right side of the bed instead of the left. I realize that willingly changing my routine allows me to deal more easily with the inevitable changes that occur in life.

# Choice

---

Each day I have the freedom to make choices. My life is about choice. When I am in doubt about a particular decision to make I can simply get quiet with myself and silently ask for guidance. I know that during the quiet times I am given the insight to make the most appropriate decisions. As I allow myself the time to go within I gain the clarity to intuitively know the best choice to make in any situation.

---

# $\mathscr{E}$xpectations

Not everyone has the same time frame as me. When I place expectations on others to stay within my guidelines, I know I am setting myself up for frustration. I know this can cause me undue and unhealthy stress. Life is too short to fret over the little things. Little things like someone showing up five minutes later than I expected or someone driving slowly in front of me when I am in a hurry. Even something like missing a flight connection is not worth stressing over. Who knows what might come from a situation such as this that may benefit my life if I am open. Today, I will consciously make an effort to relax in all situations.

# Guidance

Each moment in life is simply a memory of a time before. All that I believe to be true is based on my past experiences. There may be times I feel lonely in the present. To be as complete as I possibly can be in the present, all I need do is look over my life and realize that the times I felt most alone and afraid were when I tried to do life on my own. I felt alone and confused when I did not trust the process of life. If I get out of my own way and allow for guidance, whether it be through the words of another, an intuitive feeling or thought, or from a message in a book, I can truly know peace and happiness.

# *O*penness

I must allow myself to be open to the messages from various sources in life. So often, I try to figure things out by myself. It is by doing this I may feel alone and afraid. By simply turning my heart and attention to what is in front of me, my soul is filled and all I need is made available. I don't have to experience life alone. At all times I can be guided if I am open to this.

# Having Enough

In this moment I have all that I absolutely need. When I find myself being motivated by the fear of not having enough, I will pause, notice what I do have and move my attention to the present moment. By staying very present in the moment the fear of lack is lifted. It is through a conscious awareness my eyes can be opened to the blessings of life. It is through appreciating what I do have that makes me open to receiving more.

# All I Need

In this moment I have all I need. There may be plenty of times when I want more than what I have. My wants and desires may fill my thoughts and leave me feeling empty. And yet, if I allow myself to acknowledge all that I have, I realize that I have been provided with all that I am truly in need of. When I realize that I have been taken care of and that my needs are being met, the emptiness will leave and I will be at peace.

# Impatience

So often I find myself rushing through my day. For today I will remember to pause and give thanks for what I am experiencing. It is not about how much I accomplish at day's end. Rather, it is about how much joy I experienced and brought to the lives of others throughout the minutes and hours of the day. When I rush through my days, I will miss out on the experiences of life. My impatience denies me the chance to receive the gift of today. Today I will slow down.

# Expectations

When I place expectations on other people or situations, I am upsetting my ability to live life with serenity. What I expect from others is based on my beliefs; it is not necessarily how life should be. When I find myself getting out of balance based on what I expect of others, I will take the time to acknowledge that they have their own path to travel and it is not my place to determine how they walk their path.

# This Moment

---

Today is the only day I have. There are two ways I can perceive this information. The first is to do whatever I want without regard to what is good or right for myself and others. When I do this I may be acting irresponsibly. The second way is to live life to the fullest, appreciate each moment and be accountable and responsible for my actions towards myself and others. When I walk in love I will automatically follow the path that allows me to be responsible and accountable while living life to the fullest.

---

# rust

---

Often, there are things that will occur which I do not understand. I may find myself resisting what is going on. It is through the resistance that I create unnecessary frustration and stress. It would benefit me to trust that all is as it should be. The outcome of any situation is often based on my attitude. One of the best ways to assure I have a good outcome is to have a loving and positive attitude and to trust the process of life.

---

# Letting Go

How often do I spend my time thinking about what might or might not happen in the future? How often do I worry unnecessarily about things over which I have no control at this time? Today I will trust that my future will be exactly as it should be. Today I will release the need to control outcomes. Today I will willingly accept all that life puts in front of me.

# Clarity

I enjoy the quiet time I share with myself. In the silence of my mind and heart I can connect with my purpose in a most peaceful way. I can tune into the clarity that is meant to be mine. I give thanks for the goodness that has been bestowed upon me. I give thanks for the clarity as it unfolds.

# Love

---

With love in my life all things are possible. Everything I am experiencing is part of life's plan. I may not always understand the path I am on, but as I allow myself to trust the process, and do it with love, I can move along my path with ease.

---

# ife

Sometimes I get frustrated with what I do or don't have in my life. Everything comes to me in its' right time and place. Life shines goodness on me constantly even though I may not always acknowledge this. Each moment is my opportunity to open my heart to life and all its' goodness. Each moment is my opportunity to trust in the process. When I trust I know my needs are met.

# reams

All of us have dreams. Some are large, some are small. There are some dreams I have never taken action on. It could be the desire to take acting    classes, or learn to skydive, go on a cruise, or travel to some exotic, far away place. Whatever my heart's desire is, I will take one step towards living that dream. The step could be something as simple as picking up a brochure from a travel agency or calling the local college to find out when the next drama class begins. However small the step is, I commit to taking the action today.

# Creativity

Creativity occurs when I let life flow. When I try to take control of the creative process, I am blocking the way. I need to make room for whatever comes so that I may receive insights. Today I will take the time to savor every moment. I will breathe deeply of the bounty of life. I will take time to smell the roses and walk in nature. For it is in communion with nature I can connect with my deepest level of creativity. Creativity is simply life working through me.

# Know Myself

There have been times in the past I feared knowing who I am. This is no longer true. I have learned that in silence I come to know my true self. So much is revealed to me when I am quiet within myself. Today, I relish the opportunities to know and love myself completely. Today I enjoy every expression of who I am.

# Reflection

There are many times in life that what I see in another is simply a reflection of myself. If I see anger, hostility, aggression and lack of love in another it is usually fear within me that is being reflected. It benefits me to look within, to see if perhaps these are parts of myself I need to heal. By asking for my eyes to be open and my heart to be willing, I can move from a place of fear to a place of love. By moving in love I can truly share the gifts of life with others.

# Giving My Best

To live a complete life I must give my best to every encounter I have. With every person I cross paths with, may each encounter be complete as we part our ways on the physical realm. May I give all the love, all the honesty, all the joy that I am capable of giving to another in each moment that I am with them. May I leave no stone unturned, no thought unsaid, no words unspoken to those I love so that each relationship is complete at all times.

# ourage

Fear is something that can immobilize me. Courage is not the absence of fear. Courage is the ability to acknowledge fear and walk through it anyway. In looking back over my life, I realize it was during my times of greatest fear that moving into action helped me get to the other side. When I am in fear all I need to do is ask for guidance through tough situations. It is through the process of trust that I can find the courage to walk through my fears.

# Guidance

Each day I will ask to be guided. Although I know there is a guiding force in my life, I sometimes find myself resisting what may be put in front of me. What I truly ask, and am in need of, is the wisdom to be open to what life's plan for me and others is. The greatest gift I can give is the acceptance of what life has in store for me and for them.

# urpose

Each day is an opportunity to tune into a deeper level to my purpose in life. Although I may think my purpose has something to do with the material world, in all reality, my only purpose in life is to come from a place of love and joy. In doing so, I find that all confusion as to why I was put on this earth lifts from my mind, heart and soul.

# Ego

Often my ego will try to convince me I should be doing something other than what I am doing. In this world, everyone is a messenger. Some carry the message of goodness, for others this is not so. I desire to carry the message of love, kindness, goodness and joy. Any way that I am delivering the message is exactly how it should be done. It could be one-on-one situations or it could be through working with large groups. When I doubt myself, it is the ego that is telling me that I am not doing what I "should" be doing. When I am truly walking my path every moment is a moment of teaching for myself and others.

# Being My Best

In life, the best I can do is the best I can do. I don't need to stress over what I could have done yesterday or what I can do tomorrow. All I can do is be present in the moment and live each moment to the fullest. With a conscious awareness of what is right and appropriate, I know I am always doing my very best.

# This Moment

Each moment is a new opportunity to breathe in the goodness of life. Each moment I can make a loving difference in the life of another. Each moment I can do something to heal the earth. Each moment I can realize that this is the only time I have. Each moment I can consciously choose to take the necessary steps to live fully.

# Happiness

People often insist that in order to be happy we must constantly strive to have bigger, better, more. In reality it is not about continually obtaining and wanting more. Happiness is about being grateful for what I have at any given moment. It is in the ability to be truly grateful for whatever is in my life that I will find a deeper level of joy and happiness. When I am feeling unhappy, all I have to do is stop and reflect on what I have to be grateful for. By doing this, I will then be able to move back to a place of happiness and joy.

# Self-Esteem

Sometimes I may not feel like I am doing all I should be doing. When this happens my self-esteem may be low. In reality, the way to keep my self-esteem at a good level is to be connected with my purpose in life. When I am connected with my purpose I know in my heart I always have enough of everything. I know that I am just fine the way I am.

# Achievement

So often I get hung up on what I think I should be doing rather than just living in the moment. I may try desperately to achieve something I think will make me more valuable to others and in the process I    forget that I am valuable just as I am. I do not have to chase after anything. All my needs are being met. I am being taken care of through the process of life. I am constantly blessed with inspiring thoughts and creative ideas. It is up to me to honor my life by taking appropriate action on these thoughts and ideas. By doing this I achieve all that I am meant to.

# orth

My worth is not determined by my outward accomplishments. My worth has already been determined by the fact I am alive. The only measuring stick I need is love and understanding. Beyond that, most things are illusions.

# reativity

Creativity is in me at all times. When I feel blocked or uncreative it could be that I am too focused on outcomes. All I need to do is turn my thoughts to the creative process and my energy is open. It may be that I need to connect with my creativity by getting close to nature. It may be that I need to have the courage to change my routines and trust that all will work out as it should. In this moment I turn my thoughts to the guidance of my creative energy.

# *S*uccess

Throughout my life I have determined what success means. As I have grown and changed, my definition has also changed. As I become a more complete person I realize that success today is not necessarily what I thought it would be yesterday. Today the greatest success I can experience is to reach a level of love, willingness and acceptance of the process of my life.

# Being Okay

---

It is okay for me to not feel "on top of the world" every day. Some days the best I can do is to simply put one foot in front of the other. When I am going through extremely painful experiences it is important for me not to stuff my pain. I will allow myself to feel my feelings and ask for the guidance to get me through my process. I will allow others to see my pain and help me to get to the other side. I will allow myself to be vulnerable. I will allow myself to be human.

---

# Kindness To Myself

I will treat myself with kindness throughout the day. I will notice what I am putting into my mind, body and spirit. I will notice if I am treating myself with love and kindness on all levels. At any moment in my day I can change what I am doing to be more loving to myself and others. I make a conscious choice to be kind throughout the day with all I come in contact.

# Solitude

---

Often I get so caught up in accomplishing things that I forget to take time just to be. When is the last time I simply allowed myself to sit in a quiet space with no other purpose than to be? Today I will take the time to sit quietly with myself. Time to enjoy the quietness of solitude. Time to relax in the moment. Time to connect with myself and my intended path.

---

# Being Alone

There are times I need to be alone with no distractions. So often in life, I keep myself excessively busy to avoid my own thoughts, feelings and emotions. Sometimes I must simply slow down, breathe deep, and get to know who I really am. Today, I will give myself permission to have quiet time.

# elaxing

When I get caught up in the hustle and bustle of life I will consciously take the time to relax. So often, I get into the mindset that there just isn't enough time to do all that I need to do. In reality, I have all the time necessary to complete everything I must do. It may just be that my ego is trying to defeat the balance of life by telling me that I am not doing what I must. The only thing I need do in life to be happy is to be present in the moment. The more I take time to stay balanced, the more I will accomplish all that I am intended to.

# Life's Process

---

Sometimes I might get frustrated because I do not understand the process of life. In reality, I already know everything I need to. The knowledge will be revealed at the right time and right place. As I am ready, the knowledge will unfold and I will remember that which I am intended to know.

---

# Experience

Whatever I want to experience in my life I must be willing to teach. If I want to experience love, I must teach love. If I want to experience peace, I must teach peace. If I want to experience joy, I must teach joy. The most powerful way to teach is through my actions. When my actions match my words I am teaching my truth.

# ntegrity

The most empowering way for me to live my life is with integrity. Integrity is about being whole and complete. When I am doing this I have balance in my heart and mind. I intuitively know if I am living with integrity. The purest way to achieve this is when my words and my actions match.

# *D*reams

---

Whatever my dreams and goals, it is up to me to take action on them. Often what holds me back from taking action is fear. Fear of failure, of success, of rejection, of acceptance, or of making a mistake. The only mistake I can truly make is to not take action on my dreams. In my heart, I know that when I allow myself to be guided all my actions will be appropriate and move me closer to the fruition of my dreams and my life's path. May I accept life's guidance now and always.

---

# Teaching

I can only teach others what I believe to be true. If I believe life is good then I can teach good. If I believe life to be bad then I will teach the lessons of sorrow and despair. I must look within my heart to know what is true. What is the legacy I choose to pass on to others?

# urpose

There are times I put so much effort in trying to figure out why I am here and what I am supposed to be doing. All around me there are reminders. It is all very simple. I only have to put one foot in front of the other and trust the process of life and everything will be revealed. I need only open my eyes and heart to a higher level of awareness to realize there are people all around me who are in pain. There is anger, violence, and hostility destroying people's lives. My purpose is to merely touch the lives of as many people as I can in a loving way.

# Growth

---

As I grow and develop, I develop into who I am meant to be. It is through the resistance of that growth, through the resistance of the emergence of who I am, that I experience pain. When I allow life to guide me I realize that anywhere I am and anything I experience, is exactly where I need to be.

---

# Flow

There may be times I get frustrated with the pace of my life. Maybe I don't think things are moving along quickly enough, or maybe I think things are happening too quickly. To have serenity and balance in my life, I must remember that life is happening at just the pace it is intended. The best I can do is to take action on my hopes and dreams and let go of the outcome. I cannot force the flow of how things should be, I can only be accountable for my actions. For today, I take full responsibility for my actions. For today, I let life flow.

# Fear

When I walk in fear it simply means I have forgotten. Forgotten that in the past the way through fear was not to deny it, but rather to acknowledge it and be willing to walk through it anyway. The times I was able to gracefully get to the other side of fear was when I allowed myself to trust the process of life. Also, when I allowed the love of others to guide me through. I do not have to do life alone. I can turn to the goodness of friends, family and co-workers for loving guidance.

# Growth

As I grow and change, I realize things that may have been of interest to me in the past may no longer hold that same appeal. It is okay to let go of those things that no longer work in my life, those things that no longer bring satisfaction and joy. Today what brings satisfaction and joy is walking my path in life, doing what is a part of my life's work. I trust that each day I will grow in ways that are loving and kind.

# Purpose

There are occasions I may search for my purpose and meaning in life. When I pay attention I realize it has been made abundantly clear. My role is to live with love and joy. My purpose is to be present in the moment and to connect with others in a loving way. My purpose is to live each moment with gratitude and to share goodness with others. For today I live my purpose.

# Completeness

As I reflect on my life and all I have done or not done, do I feel complete? Each moment I have the opportunity to make my life complete through my thoughts and actions. My life is whole when I move in love and harmony. When I speak kind words and take kind actions towards all I come in contact with then I am complete. It is up to me in each moment to make my life whole. By consciously accepting my path and purpose I am complete, whole and fulfilled.

# Giving

I cannot give what I do not have. To give love, I must have love. To give happiness I must have happiness. To give freedom, I must have freedom. To give the wisdom of taking risks to another, I must have taken risks. It doesn't matter what the outward circumstances are. It is what is going on inside. To give to others I must first know that I have this inside. And with love in my heart all things are possible.

# nger

Anger at another person can be unhealthy for me, even when I consider my anger to be justified. Anger simply means that I have a different set of values and beliefs than someone else. Their beliefs are not necessarily bad or wrong, they are simply different. For today, when I find I am getting angry with others, I will stop myself and send kind and loving thoughts their way.

# chievement

So often I try to achieve far too much in any given period of time. Today I will take time to relax, rest and regroup. It is not necessary for me to constantly be achieving. Sometimes the greatest gift I can give to myself and others is to just be.

# hoice

With each moment that passes I have the opportunity to make a positive difference in someone's life. It is up to me, in the moment-by-moment decisions I make as to what I contribute to the life of another. I ask for guidance to take the right action at all times. I ask that I have the willingness to be a loving and giving person.

# Gratitude

---

Each day I have so much to be grateful for. In the rush of my day I may forget the good that surrounds me. Today, and every day, I will take the time to look for all that is good in my life. I know that when I focus on what is good, and what is right, the goodness will multiply.

---

# Anger And Resentment

It is important to let go of the anger and resentment I hold towards others. These emotions usually crop up when another person does not act or respond in the way I think they should. I need to remember that not everyone has the same values as I do, nor will they respond to situations like I do. What I do know is that the higher my expectations, the lower my peace of mind. Today, when I find myself getting angry, I will notice what expectations are not being met or what fears I may be experiencing. I will ask for guidance to help me walk through my fear, anger and resentment in order to become a kinder and more loving person.

# Being Open

If I keep myself open to the experiences and opportunities of life, all I need is provided for. There may be times I feel alone, confused or afraid. By keeping my mind and heart open I soon realize that everything and everyone I need are always present. People are placed in my life to enjoy more meaning and fulfillment. All I need to do is be willing, open and aware.

# Resentments

Resentments play havoc on my body, mind and soul. They cause me to harm myself in subtle, and sometimes not so subtle, ways. Resentments prevent me from living life to the fullest. By forgiving others, I can learn to live life in a loving and compassionate way.

# Frustrations

Sometimes I get frustrated with the way my day is going. Perhaps others are not moving at the pace I think they should. Or there is more traffic than I had hoped. Maybe I don't have as much money as I think I should have. At times like these I will take a moment to remember there is a plan for my life. It is just that all has not been revealed. I will trust the process and realize my path is moving in the direction that is best for me.

# Fear

Fear can appear even though I know I am on the right path in life, I am doing the right things and making the most appropriate choices. Fear of loss, of not having enough money, of losing credibility, of failure, or of making a mistake. During these times, all I have to do is turn to a power greater than myself to ask for the strength and guidance to do what I know in my heart is the right thing. Often, fear is based on what my ego believes to be true, not on reality. By asking for right guidance the fear will be lifted.

# Being Thankful

---

The more I can focus on what I have to be thankful for the easier it is for me to notice what I have to be thankful for. There is abundance and happiness all around me. There are good people everywhere. All I need to do is open my eyes to see and open my heart to love. If I cannot open my eyes and heart, I will ask for the willingness to be willing to be open.

---

# ℛesentments

Life is far too short to carry resentments around in my mind and heart. Each day I will notice if I am carrying any resentments and make sure to release them as soon as I notice them. I will forgive others and myself for any indiscretions I may have felt, or currently feel. This does not mean I must be a doormat for others. It simply means I can live a loving and forgiving life.

# Gratitude

It is important to be thankful. To give thanks for what is in my life is the greatest gift I can give back to life. When I am so focused on what I do not have and am not thankful, it is difficult for goodness to enter into my heart. Today I will give thanks for all the blessings in my life. If I find this difficult I will remember to be grateful for the small things. Something as simple as the fact that today I woke up and was able to get out of bed. I have a bed to sleep in. I have a roof over my head. Maybe it is to acknowledge a special friendship. By being grateful of what is good in life I will be blessed with more.

# nitiative

Today I will take the initiative to do something I have been putting off for some time. It could be calling a friend I haven't talked to in awhile, cleaning out a closet that I have avoided organizing, or writing a letter to a loved one. I will take the initiative to do something that will give me a sense of satisfaction and possibly bring pleasure to someone else. Today, no matter what, I commit to an action.

# Being Present

When I am not focused on the present moment I am missing the essence of life. The key to true happiness is to stay completely present in this very moment. It is important to be present in the painful and uncomfortable moments as well as those that are happy and joyful. Regardless of what I am doing, when I am living in the moment, a loving memory can be created. Even during times of pain, at some point, the memories will be loving if I am open. I am grateful for this moment.

# Gratitude

For today I will breathe life into all my experiences. I will be grateful for anything that comes my way, no matter how pleasant, no matter how painful. Although I may not understand all I am experiencing in this moment, I know that there is a plan for my life. With many experiences there will be pain and confusion. Misery, however, is optional. By trusting the process, all things are made clear and I am able to walk through the pain put in front of me. By expressing gratitude for all the blessings I have, the pain is more tolerable and easier to accept. I ask for the willingness to walk through life's obstacles and show gratitude in all I do.

# Fear Of Self

At times I hesitate letting others know who I am or how I really feel out of fear they may not like me or they will reject me. If I am hiding who I am out of fear, then I am not giving others the opportunity to know the real me. When I trust the process of life, and realize who I am is a unique individual with a purpose for being here, I can be comforted in knowing who I am is good. Today I will take comfort in knowing I am here to bring fullness to the lives of others by being true to who I am.

# Love

One of the greatest fears known to mankind is the fear of not being loved. This fear can impact all areas of our lives. To experience something from another, I must first being willing to give it. When I am coming from a place of love, when I am staying present in this very moment, when I am in a place of being of service to others and coming from my heart, any feeling of not being loved will disappear.

In closing...

In each moment you can create your
**Message of Hope.**

## About Kathleen Gage

Described by many as one of the most inspirational speakers alive, Kathleen Gage has traveled throughout the world inspiring thousands in both the public and private sector through her speaking, training, consulting and writing.

In her teens and early twenties Kathleen made choices that took her from a comfortable middleclass upbringing to a life of homelessness and being unemployable. Rising above insurmountable odds Kathleen has become a successful business owner, respected leader in her field and community leader.

With a deep thirst for inner knowledge, Kathleen traveled throughout the world gaining insights that she willingly shares with others. Living for extended periods of time on the West Bank of Israel and Mexico, overcoming a bout with paralysis at a young age and living through the great quake of 1985 in

Mexico City, Kathleen has a unique understanding of the delicate balance of life.

Kathleen Gage has dedicated her life to assisting others in creating a better quality of life through common sense, a commitment to self, spirituality, and the right attitude.

To book Kathleen Gage for your next engagement contact the author at

Turning Point, Inc.
563 East Stratford Drive
Salt Lake City, Utah 84106

801.466.3630
www.turningpointpresents.com
turningpoint@utah-inter.net

# Give the Gift of Hope
## Check your leading bookstore or order here

Yes, I Want_____ Copies of **Message of Hope** at $10.95 each, plus $2 shipping per book (Utah residents please add .72 sales tax per book). Canadian orders must be accompanied by a postal money order in U.S. funds. Allow 15 days for delivery.

My check or money order for $_____ is enclosed.

Name:

Organization:

Address:

City/State/Zip:

Phone:

Email:

**Please make your check payable and return to:**
**Turning Point, Inc.**
**563 East Stratford Drive**
**Salt Lake City , Utah 84106**

Phone: 801.466.3630 Fax: 801.467.4694 Email: turningpoint@utah-inter.net
www.turningpointpresents.com

**Discounts for quantity sales. Call for information.**